WONDERFUL
PRAGUE

Edizioni **KINA Italia / L.E.G.O.**

Historical Introduction

1. *Kraner's Fountain (known as the monument to Emperor Frantisek II)*
2. *Hanavský's pavilion, in neo-baroque style, was built in 1891 for the Universal Exposition and later moved to the Letná Hill (at the outskirts of the city) in 1898.*
3. *Týn Church and the sculpture dedicated to Jas Hun*
4. *The Castle from the Moldava river*

Page 2-3 Entrance to the Old Town from Charles Bridge

The origins of Prague date to the second half of the 6th century AD, when some Slavonic tribes settled in the Vltava Valley and founded the first villages from which the city developed. Around the 7th century the Přemyslovci tribe assumed supremacy over the others, starting a dynasty that will reign over the region for 400 years. Between the end of the 9th and the beginning of the 10th century, the Přemyslovci built two fortresses: Prague's Castle and the Vyšehrad Fort, set on a rock at a short distance from the present city. The former was founded by Borivoj, the first Přemysl prince to be baptized, by hand of the Saints Cyril and Methodius who at the time were preaching the Christian doctrine in the area. Christianity spread quickly, thanks also to the example of the prince, who had a church dedicated to the Virgin Mary built inside the fortress. Some years later (about 920), his successor Vratislav I ordered the construction in the same place of the Saint George Church. Venceslas too, grandson of Borivoj, promoted the Christian religion; he was killed on order of his brother Boleslav in 935, and canonized, soon becoming one of the most relevant names in the history of Prague. The construction within the walls of the castle of the Saint Vitus Rotunda, over which the chapel dedicated to the saint prince will be built, is due to him. In Prague, named Bishopric in 973, the political power of the princes is already tightly bound to religion, as demonstrated by the Edict of 1039, by which Břetislav I orders his subjects to convert to Christianity. In 1085 Vratislav II, risen to the throne in 1061, is nominated king by Henry IV, Emperor of the Holy Roman German Empire, to which already in the 10th century Bohemia had declared itself vassal. In the 12th century, above all during the reign of Vladislav II (1140-1173), commerce and business greatly developed in the city, in particular thanks to Jewish and German merchants who settled in the area of the Old Town Square. In this period romanesque art flourishes, leaving rich examples throughout the city. Around 1170, the first stone bridge of the city, Judith Bridge, is completed, joining the two banks of the Vltava. Successor to Venceslas I, the king Přemysl Otakar II (1253-1278) in 1257 grants the status of city to the settlements on the left bank of the Vltava, renaming the area Malá Strana (Small Neighborhood), as distinguished from the Old Town on the right bank, that in 1287 will be finally nominated capital of the kingdom. In 1278 Otakar dies in the battle of Marchfeld fought against Rudolf of Hapsbourg, loosing much of his territories. His son Venceslas II takes the throne, maintaining power only over Bohemia and Moravia. In 1305 he is succeeded by the last king of the Přemysl dynasty, Venceslas III, who is killed just the year after. From the marriage of his daughter Elisabeth to John of Luxembourg, Bohemia's king, Charles is born, who will be crowned as Charles I in 1346, and as Charles IV, Emperor of the Holy Roman German Empire in 1355. Under his rule (1346-1378), Prague, that had been granted its own Municipality in 1338, became imperial residence. The city experiences then a period of great growth in all the aspects of its life, from economy to architecture and arts. By order of the Emperor, the castle was reconstructed, the building of the Great Saint Vitus Cathedral begun, Charles Bridge was completed and Prague's Bishop Residence become an Archbishopric Palace. Several convents were founded, together with the first German University and the Carolinum College. A new section of city is born, New Town. Politically, Charles IV obtains a truly important change with the Golden Bull of 1356, that establishes, among other things, the independence of the Czech Kingdom from the Empire and bestows on the King of Bohemia the title of First Lay Elector of the Empire. A well different destiny befalls on the city during the reign of Venceslas IV, succeeded to the father in 1378. After the Emperor Sigismund decided not to reside in the city, Prague is swept in 1380 by a plague: the disease causes a profound economic crisis that affects more severely the lower classes. In 1389 a revolt starts against the Jews, accused of having poisoned the city's

water. From that moment Prague lives a period of bitter social conflicts, that soon take on a religious connotation. Crucial character in this context is Jan Hus, a Bohemian preacher who attacks the Church's corruption, gathering support in all social classes. In Prague he spreads his ideas from the Bethlehem's Chapel, that becomes the center of the Hussite reform.

Initially he was supported also by Venceslas, motivated by religious and political opportunity, but after 1412, year in which Hus is excommunicated, the King is forced to ask him to leave the city. Strong of his own beliefs and to assert his ideal of a Christian Church, Hus decides to participate to the Constance Council, to which the Emperor also takes part. However he is jailed and burned at the stake for heresy. Executed in 1415, the sentence has the sole result of making Hus a national hero to the eyes of the Czech population. The social unrest, sharpened by the crowning of Sigismund, breaks out with the assault on the New City Hall and the defenestration of two catholic Town Councilors. The event marks the beginning of the Hussite Wars, conducted against the catholic troops of the Emperor, but also expressed in a conflict within the Hussites themselves, divided between moderate (Utraquists) and radicals (Taborists). The latter are finally defeated in the battle of Lipany in 1434, when the moderates recognize the authority of Sigismund. In 1448 George of Podebrady, chief of the Utraquist troops, occupies Prague and ten years after becomes the first Hussite king of Bohemia. Excommunicated by the

1. View of the city
2. Stavovské Theater
3. The elegant façade in Art Nouveau style of the Economy Ministry Palace
4. Façade of St. Salvator Church
5. Aerial view of Prague

Church, he reigns till 1471, creating for the city a new period of greatness that continues with his successor Wladislav II of Jagellon. The religious battles do not end, though, as in fact they become more violent in 1483. King Louis of Jagellon is crowned in 1516; he finally dies in the battle of Mohács (1526), leaving to the Hapsbourg dynasty the crown of Bohemia. During the reigns of Ferdinand I, Maximilian II and Rudolf II, Prague returned to be politically important as it became once more the imperial city, experiencing then an artistic and cultural renaissance that had no equals in other European cities, in spite of its coming often at odds with the catholic absolutism imposed to the Czechs and by them never tolerated. In 1618, two catholic officials were defenestrated from the halls of the Castle: it is the beginning of the 30 Years War, that ends for the Hussites with their final defeat by catholic troops. The war was concluded with the White Mountain battle in 1620, that marked for Bohemia the loss of any political and religious privilege. The Hapsbourg's rule over Bohemia was definitely set with the Westphalia Peace treaty, in 1648. Up to the 19th century Prague lived a period of prosperity, although the nationalist feelings of the population were never extinguished: the Reformers played a fundamental role in promoting the language and the Czech national culture. In 1848 a popular revolt brings about the concession of some fundamental rights. With the armistice of 1918, Czechoslovakia declares its independence and elects Tomáš Garyk Masaryk President of the Republic. In 1935 his successor, Edward Beneš, signs an alliance agreement with the Soviets Union, but in 1938, after the ratification of the Munich Pact that assigns to the Hitler's Germany a substantial part of the country, the President flees to London where he heads the Resistance. In 1945, the people of Prague took over and welcomed the return of Beneš and the Red Army. Three years later the Communist Party assumes the power with Klement Gottwald, who introduc-

es in the country Stalin's rule. In 1968 Alexander Dubček, First Secretary of the Socialist Czech Republic, initiates a set of reforms that are at the beginning of the Spring of Prague, drowned in blood by the troops of Warsaw Pact that occupy the city. While Gustav Husák is governing the country, in 1977, the civil rights manifesto Charta 77 is published. The pressure for freedom is getting progressively stronger: in 1989 great public demonstrations take place in Prague, finally resulting in the election of Václav Havel to the Presidency. It is the "Velvet Revolution", that will bring two years later to the departure of Russian occupation troops and the recognition of civil and political rights. In 1993 Prague is the capital of the new Czech Republic, independent and separate from the Slovak state.

1. *View of the City Hall Tower*
2. *Spectacular view St. Nicholas Church, City Hall tower and Týn Church in the background*

Old Town Square

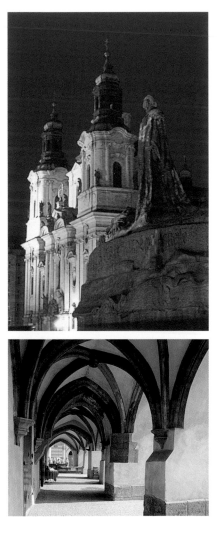

Panoramas of the Old Town Square with the Virgin Mary of Týn Church and the memorial monument to the Reformer Jan Hus

True outdoors museum of Prague's history and architecture, the Square may be considered the original core of the whole city. Right here, in fact, settled in the 10-11th century the flourishing merchant communities that came from all over Europe, marking with their presence throughout the century the economic and cultural life of Prague. Since the 16th century the Old Town Square has been the place of the main city market, soon becoming the center of the most important neighborhood and enriched in several periods by new houses, palaces and monuments, many of them still remaining to these days. Declared City at the beginning of the 13th century, Prague is granted only a century later the right to have her own Municipality, represented by the palace built in this very Square, which became from that moment also the political heart of the city. Starting from the Powder Portal, built at the end of the 15th century on the model of the Old Town Tower that 100 years before Peter Parléř added to Charles Bridge (considered later), the Square is reached through the ancient Celetná Street, that ends at the south-east corner, dominated by the presence of the Týn Church.

Dedicated to the Virgin Mary and second in importance only to Saint Vitus Cathedral, this church's construction was initiated in 1365 on the site of a more ancient temple and continued till the second half of the 15th century. From that moment till 1620, date of the White Mountain battle, it has been the center of Hussite preaching. After the victory of the Catholics on the Reformers, the church underwent important alterations, particularly outside. The Golden Chalice that was decorating the façade to represent Hussite faith was melted and the metal used to make the Virgin sculpture, still displayed today. The interiors were redecorated in baroque style. Saint Mary of Týn, besides the tomb of the astronomer Tycho Brahe, preserves several remarkable examples of picture and sculpture. Walking beyond the two buildings facing the church (Týn House and White Unicorn House, of the 15th and 18th century, respectively) and the medieval Stone Bell House, with its beautiful gothic façade, the visitor comes up to the imposing rococo palace Golz-Kinský. Built in the second half of the 18th century, it displays on its monumental façade rich stucco decorations and allegoric statues representing the four elements. The area in front of it is dominated by the monument to Jan Hus, created at the beginning of the 1900 by the Czech sculptor Vladislav Saloun in the date of the 5th centennial of the Reformer's death, burned at the stake for heresy in 1415 and later become symbol of national unity. The majestic figure of the hero is set above the groups that the artist has designed to display the history of the Hussites, marked first by victory and then by exile, and the symbol of hope for the Czech

nation, represented by a mother with her son. On the north-east side of the square are lined palaces constructed between the end of the 19th and the beginning of the 20th century, in replacement of older buildings demolished in the project of reclamation of the old Jewish neighborhood that used to be just beyond that area (considered later). Worth of attention is the palace presently housing the Economy Ministry, built in 1898, with its beautiful Art Nouveau façade. At its side are an elegant building of 16th century origin (ex Saint Paul's convent), and a palace in neo-baroque style built at the beginning of this century. Right beyond, on the right (in the northwest corner) is found Saint Nicholas, among the oldest and historically most important churches of the city (considered later). The west side includes charming greens, where often are stationed the

View of the sculptures in Liberty style, created by the sculptor Vladislav Saloun, dedicated to Jan Hus, leader of the Reformers

carriages and colorful souvenir stands for the tourists. The garden ends at the south corner with the Old Town Municipality Tower, easily recognized because of the people that at all times crowd around it and, more importantly, the famous astronomic Horologe. The ancient City Hall is in fact composed of several buildings, in different period and style, that go from the tower to the house called "U Minuty", famous for its graffiti façade.

When in 1338, the year king John of Luxembourg granted the city the right

1. *The inscription "Praga caput regni" in the City Hall of the Old Town and the window of the Wedding Hall*
2. *Týn Church and the sculpture dedicated to Jas Hun*
3. *The Old Town Square*
4. *View of the Old Town Square with the city Hall and the Týn Church*

to build its own Municipality, the site chosen was the Wolfin of Kamen House, at the corner of the square. Only 30 years after the tower was added, and in 1381 a corner chapel was included, with a bow window of five elegant stained glass panels and splendid interior decorations. In the lower part of the tower (entering through its graceful gothic portal, the visitor can take the stairs leading up to the panoramic gallery) is located the famous Astronomic Horologe, made in 1410 and improved several times till 1590. On the clock's face, the Earth is represented, according to the beliefs of the time, at the center of the universe, surrounded by the other planets that rotate around it. From 8 a.m.to9 p.m., at the strike of the hour, a complex mechanism in the clock clicks and moves the figure representing Death (on the right of the face), which turns over the sand-clock, symbolizing the passing of life, and pulls a rope held in its right hand, causing two tiny windows above the clock to open: a procession of Apostles led by Saint Peter then crosses the face. At the end of the procession the windows close and a rooster above marks the end of the activity with its crowing. At the sides of the clock face are placed three figures that also get in motion when the hour strikes: the Turk, Vanity and Greed. Under the clock is represented the calendar of the zodiac signs (19th century). The tower has at its sides two other Municipality buildings: Kriz House, with its stunning gratings topped by the town's insignia, bearing the words "Praga caput regni", and the refined window of the Council Hall (16th century); Mikes House and the Minute House, where lived Franz Kafka, decorated with elaborated graffiti of biblical inspiration.

1. *The Old Town Square is always animated by stands of any kind and unusual outdoor exhibitions*
2. *The astronomic Horologe, with the allegoric images of the months, created by Josef Mánes*
3. *View of the Old Town Square*

In front of the City Hall, on the south side of the square between Celetná and Zelezná Streets, is a row of houses and palaces in romanesque and gothic style, with colorful names. Storch House, built in the 19th century over an older gothic palace, still displays on its façade a painting of the period depicting Saint Venceslas on a horse. The Stone Ram House shows a beautiful relief, over the 16th century portal, representing a ram with a single horn, like a unicorn. Follow the Stone Table House, of the 14th century, the Poor Unhappy Man House, with romanesque foundations, and the Golden Unicorn house, originally of the 12th century. Beyond Zelezná Street rises a set of houses with porticos (The Storks, The Red Fox, The Blue Star), connected to the 1400's Ochs House by the narrow Melantrichova passage that opens onto a quaint little alley of the Old Town.

1. The renaissance "U Minuty" House, decorated with graffiti representing mythological scenes
2. Image of the majestic gothic City Hall Tower
3. The quaint Melantrichova passage

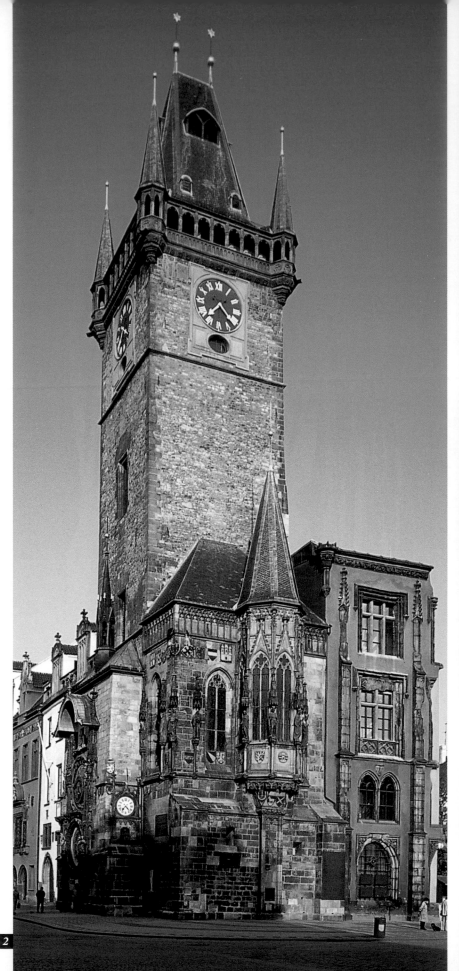

Saint Nicholas

A first church dedicated to Saint Nicholas, patron of the merchants, was already built on this site in gothic style, during the 13th century. It had been offered by the German merchants community which had started settling in this part of the city from the preceding century. Later the church was modified and partially reconstructed several times, till the early 1700, when it was entirely rebuilt in baroque style on a project by Kilian Dientzenhofer, between 1732 and 1737. Assigned to the Benedictine monastery in the 17th century and presently belonging to the Czech Hussite Church, the imposing building has been occupied during its history also by lay institutions. In fact, for a time in the 13th century, it became headquarters of the Municipality, as an actual City Hall was yet to be built; later (after 1781, when Joseph II ordered the suppression of several monasteries) it was used as archive and then as Concert Hall. The rich sculpture decoration of the outside is balanced by the surprising architectural lines and splendid decoration of the interior, in particular the frescos representing Saint Nicholas stories, that are painted on the dome.

Views and details of the St Nicholas Church, overlooking the northern part of the Old Town

Old Town

Grown around the famous square over the centuries, this is one of the quaintest neighborhoods in Prague, crossed by tiny alleys and large avenues, studded with important monuments, stores of ancient tradition, cafes and restaurants of unspoiled charm. Next to the Powder Portal is located the most renowned Liberty palace of the city: the Town Hall. Its front is decorated by a great mosaic and the interiors include many rooms splendidly appointed in that style; the largest and most beautiful of all being the Smetana Hall, the famous auditorium with its great glass dome. Passing through the Powder Portal, the visitor takes Celetná Street, reaches the Black Madonna House, a cubist building, and turns left onto the Ovochný thr., at which end rise the 1700's Theater of the General States, dedicated to Mozart. On the right is the Carolinum, heart of the University founded in the 14th century by Charles IV, still preserving the bow window in gothic style. Leaving on the right Zelezná Street, the way takes toward the Saint Gaul Church (founded in the 13th century), at the core of a very lively neighborhood, and then toward the House of the Two Golden Bears, with its precious renaissance portal. Here, turning right, one can return toward the Malé Náměstí, with at the center a well of the 16 century. On its side is the Rott House, where is lo-

1. *Hotel in the Old Town*
2-4. *Typical signs on houses*
3. *The Golden Well House*
5. *The Three Violins House*
6. *Sculpted decoration of the walls of a residence*
7. *A typical pub*

cated one of the most ancient hardware shops of the city, decorated with graffiti and paintings (19th century) representing the tools sold inside. From the square, turning left, one walks in Karlova (Charles Avenue), a colorful way opened in the 12th century, lined with some of the most beautiful gothic and renaissance houses in Prague. In particular is worth of notice the Golden Well house, with its front decorated with stucco statues representing the Virgin and Saints.

After a short walk, the visitor turns left in Husova, where the ancient Saint Giles Church is found, with its elegant baroque interior, and then turns right at Bethlehem Chapel, modern remake of the 13th century temple where Jan Hus used to preach. From here, reached the Ethnographic Museum Náprstek, the tourist may turn right in Liliová and then left in Anenská, keep going beyond the Saint Anne Convent, so coming to the Vltava's riverside, by the Smetana Museum, dedicated to the famous composer. Turning then back into Karlova, you reach the Knights of the Cross Square, right in front of the Tower of Charles Bridge (considered later), overlooked by the great Clementinum Complex, the ancient fortress of the Jesuits, presently housing the rich National Library. Following further up in Karlova toward the Old Town, turn left after a short walk to reach Mariánské Square, where, on the corner with Husova rises the Clam Gallas Palace, built in baroque style at the beginning of the 18th century. Easily recognized by its two portals sided by monumental Hercules statues, in its interiors it preserves wonderful fresco decorations of the period. From the palace you can return finally in the Old Town Square to conclude the visit with the stunning baroque church of Saint James, where is found the precious sepulcher of the Count Vratislav of Mitrovice.

1. St. Nicholas Church
2. The Doorway of the Clam Dallas Palace, with the sculpted giants
3. The old town square

Josefov and the Old Jewish Cemetery

Its traditions certainly very ancient, some place its origin even in 970, the Jewish community of Prague lived in the area that is today known as the Old Jewish Neighborhood from the 12th century. Isolated like a ghetto and not unlike other communities throughout Europe, the one in Prague was object for centuries of senseless and brutal anti-Semitism, carried out as expropriations, discrimination and violence that only occasionally and for short periods were interrupted by the intervention of some enlightened sovereign. Not until the reign of Joseph II of Hapsbourg (1780-1790) the Jews were allowed to finally enjoy freedom of worship (instituted in 1782) and civil rights that up to that moment were denied to them. Renamed Josefov in celebration of the great king, the ghetto became at the end the refuge of people of very humble social position, and at the end of the 19th century was almost completely destroyed for hygienic reasons. Today are remaining only the Jewish Town Hall, some synagogues (among them the Old-New one and the Pinkas Synagogues, true temple of the Jewish memory in Prague) and the Old Cemetery, indisputably one of the most suggestive places in the entire town, both for its location and the memories that it holds between its walls. Founded in the second half of the 15th century and used for buri-

als till 1787, it was always enclosed in an extremely small area, within the already tight dimensions of the ghetto. For this reason in a short time it became necessary to pile the coffins one over the other, forming several layers and crowding the tombstones to give all the community members a decent burial. Walking along the narrow path that crosses it, one is not so much stricken by the disorderly abundance of tombstones set one against the other, as he is touched by the moving appeal of this sort of sacred forest of memorials, closed in by eldertrees.

Still to these days many visitors lay notes with short personal messages, held down by a pebble on the sepulchers, inspired by a complex symbolism. Among the most famous tombs is the one of Rabbi Löw (1520-1609), the renowned philosopher and writer linked to the mythic character of the Golem.

1-2. *View of Jewish building in Maiselova Street*
3-4. *The Old Jewish Cemetery with its 12,000 tombstones*
5. *The "Ceremony Hall" building. It houses the Jewish Museum*

Schwarzenberg Palace

Majestic without being heavy, the palace that overlooks the Castle Square is one of the most fortunate example of the renaissance architecture in Prague. Its construction was commissioned by Jan of Lobkowitz to Agostino Galli and realized between 1545 and 1576. The Italian architect succeeded in blending harmoniously the standards of the Renaissance, in particular the Florentine ones, with characteristics more typical of Nordic architecture. It is clear demonstration of this the decoration of the imposing facade, covered by graffiti, that displays the ashlar motif of the diamond tip made famous by, for instance, Palazzo Pitti in Florence. While on the other hand, the three level Wimberg frontispiece is of classical Bohemian inspiration. The palace, become property of the Schwarzenberg at the beginning of the 18th century, has been Prague's Museum of Military History of since 1945. In the many rooms decorated with frescos are displayed, next to paintings of historical theme, interesting weapon collections and uniforms worn by different armies participating in the frequent wars between the period of the Slays and the First World War. A part of the Museum is dedicated to the illustration of the war strategies and tactics used by the Hussite army.

Images and details of Schwarzenberg Palace: typical example of renaissance art, it was built by the architect Agostino Galli. It houses the Military Museum

Imperial Palace

Set on heights that overlook the city, the imposing palace in Viennese rococo style that leads to the greater complex of the Castle, was designed by Nicola Pacassi during the reign of Empress Maria Theresa (1740-1780). The Italian architect joined into a single coherent and stylistically homogeneous building some pre-existing houses that had been constructed in different periods. The palace is entered through a wide court enclosed in wrought iron rail topped by the rich blazon of the Empress. The rail is held by eight pillars that also support huge copies of the Gigantomachy sculpted by lgnaz Platzer in 1768. In the court can be seen, every day at noon, the colorful ritual of the change of the guard. In the center of the palace's front opens the so-called Matthias Portal, build by the Italian architect Scamozzi at the beginning of the 17th century, that lets into the second court of the palace, surrounded by buildings of the reign of Rudolf II of Hapsbourg, later incorporated in Pacassi's project. Among the sumptuous interiors shine for elegance and wealth the Spanish Hall and the Rudolf Gallery. In the old royal stables (on the north and west side) is housed the Castle Gallery, where are preserved precious Renaissance and baroque works, once part of the rich art collection of Rudolf II.

1. A wonderful night view of the Castle
2. View of the Castle during the change of the guard
3-4. The grill gate

Archbishopric Palace

The majestic palace, with its white façade, is still today the residence of the Archbishop of Prague. It was built in the 1560's, altered in the late 17th century, and once more revised in 1732-1784 by the Bohemian architect Johann Josef Wirch, who substantially modified the original renaissance façade to the present rococo style layout, divided in three level and spaced by columns and dumb pillars. In the central body, flanked by two slightly jutting wings, the portal (also made in the 18th century) bears the insignia of the Archbishop Antonín Príchowsky, who commissioned to Wirch the remaking of the palace. Ever since its building the residence assumed an important symbolic value within the city, as a statement of the supremacy of Catholicism. In fact it was first purchased in 1562 by Ferdinand I of Hapsbourg, risen to the throne in 1526, to be destined to private residence for the catholic bishop, so celebrating the return of the Roman faith in Prague, after the violent period of the Hussite Wars. Later, as a result of the battle of the White Mountain in 1620 that concluded the war with the victory of the catholic troops over the Czech rebels, it became the Archbishopric.

1. Archbishopric Palace
2. Internal court of the Castle
3. Archbishopric Palace and St. Vitus Cathedral
4. Family insignia of the Archbishop A. Príchowsky on the façade of the Archbishop-Palace

Saint Vitus Cathedral

1. Stained glass windows representing (from left): The Virgin Mary and the Prince Spytihnév, the Holy Trinity and St. Venceslas with Charles IV
2. View of the St. Vitus Cathedral displaying the bohemian glass mosaic of the Final Judgment, above the South entrance, called Golden Portal

The majestic building dominates with its imposing body the third inner court of the Castle. Among its countless historical monuments, Prague holds dearest and most revered its Cathedral, not only for its unquestionable artistic and architectural importance, that sets it apart as the true jewel of the city, but mostly for its being the symbol of more than a millennium of its history. The original core of the cathedral was the Saint Vitus Rotunda, built in 925 on the decision of the Bohemian Prince Venceslas, and turned, after his tragic death (935) and canonization, into the romanesque church design, to welcome all the travelers coming to venerate him. The beginning of the actual construction of the monument took place only when Charles IV came to reside in Prague (made Archbishopric on his request). He, even before being nominated Emperor (1346), authorized the construction of a new cathedral in 1344, commissioning the direction to Matthew d'Arras. After the death of the French architect, was placed in charge one of the most famous and active architect of the time, the Swabian Peter Parléř, who, assisted by his sons, continued the works till the beginning of the Hussite Wars, when the construction was interrupted. The very symbol of Catholicism, the cathedral was then occupied by the Hussites in 1421. In the following period, in spite of some important additions such as the royal mausoleum, the building remained practically awaiting completion for centuries. In fact only in the second half of the 19th century, the works resumed with construction, under the direction of Joseph Mocker, of the nave, west façade and two great spires; to terminate in 1929, year of the final consecration of the cathedral.

Only in the 20th century, then, the neo-gothic west façade, decorated by a great rose-window with scenes of the Creation and three bronze portals, replaced the south façade as front entrance. The old façade, with its wonderful Golden Door and 1300's mosaic representing the Final Judgment, was designed by Parléř, as well as the tower that dominates it, built in renaissance style. The latter was crowned by a baroque dome at the end of the 18th century, work of Nicola Pacassi. The solemn interior of the cathedral, composed of three aisles with transept, choir and side chapels, is covered by a stunning gothic vault with starry ribs, demonstration of Parléř artistic mastery and sensibility. Equally precious is, in the upper part, the women's gallery (14th century) with sculptured busts of famous people. The main entrance (west front) is flanked on each side by three neo-gothic chapels with very beautiful stained glass windows of the 1900. Walking down the nave after the new vestry and the 1700's organ on the left, visitors come up to the high altar (1870), preceded by the royal mausoleum (16th century) where are buried Ferdinand I, his

wife Anne and son Maximilian II. On the left can be seen the graceful pulpit of the 17th century, while on the left of the altar (decorated by splendid wood panels, including the one with a view of Prague in the 1600) is found the imposing and richly decorated tomb of St. John Nepomuk, champion of Catholicism, completely covered with silver, from the early 18th century. Beyond it, along the right aisle, is located the 1400's Royal Oratory, decorated on the vault with a complex design of branches and connected by an enclosed passage to the near Royal Palace. Right after it, the entrance to the Cross Chapel is found, giving access to the stairs to reach the royal crypt that holds the tombs of the emperor Charles IV, his four wives and his children, as well as those of Rudolf II and other members

1. *Interiors of the Cathedral*
2. *The distinctive gothic style of the St. Vitus Cathedral*

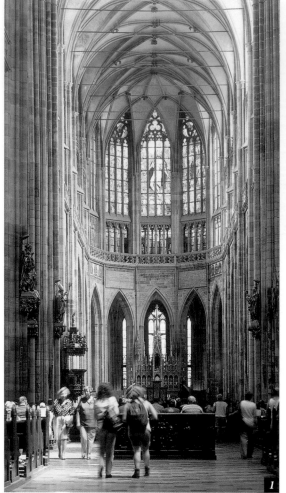

of the royal family. Inside the crypt are still preserved the remains of the original St. Vitus Rotunda and the romanesque church. Mounting the stairs, the visitor exits in front of the choir and, turning immediately on the right, reaches the most exquisite masterpiece of the church: St. Venceslas chapel. Dedicated to the saint prince killed by his brother Boleslav right in the St. Vitus Chapel, in 935, the chapel was built between 1362 and 1367 in pure gothic style by Peter Parléř. The walls, completely covered by semiprecious stones and gold decorations, in addition are enriched by the 16th century frescos depicting in the upper part stories of the life of the Saint (whose sepulcher is under the altar), and, below, stories of the life of Christ.

1. *Little quarter roofs*
2. *Golden Lane at Prague castle*
3. *Konopiště Castle (50 km away from Prague)*

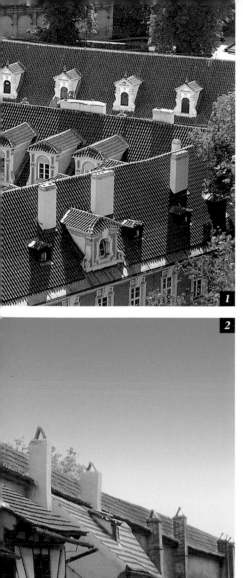

Venceslas Square

It was the Emperor Charles IV to order the creation of this large square, used for the horse market and forming, together with the other two very vast areas (Charles Square and Hay Square), the commercial core of the New Town, founded by the sovereign in 1348. Since then the square has been changed in its architectural layout, but in many ways it has maintained and developed its commercial spirit, as one can see from the shops, department stores, cafes and restaurants that open on it or into the underground passages, continuously and vivaciously animated. For the inhabitants of Prague Venceslas Square (as it was renamed after the revolution of 1848) it has a more than symbolic importance, since it has been the vital theater of the historical events most relevant to the city, up to the 1968 insurrection against the Soviet tanks that invaded the Prague in the sadly famous Prague Spring, resulting in the extreme sacrifice of young Jan Palach in January of the following year, and finally the social unrest of November 1989 and its "velvet revolution", with the consequent election to the presidency of the Republic of the ex-dissident Václav Havel. In each of these event, the huge space, with its 750 x 60 meter area, has gathered immense crowds, come together to fight, protest, express their grief and their will to live in freedom. Symbols

1. *Detail of the Art Nouveau Evropa Hotel*
2. *View of the National Museum*
3. *Venceslas Square. From 1348 also been known as "The Horse Market", today is surrounded by commercial and residential buildings. The great equestrian statue of the Duke Venceslas with the four Saints. Patrons of the Country stands out*

of this constant presence and unrelenting will of the people is the equestrian monument of Saint Venceslas and the four patrons of Bohemia that is placed at the entrance of the square. And so is the moving "monument" to the victims of communism, in fact a simple flower and candle arrangement that holds the photographs brought by the citizen in memory of those who lost their life in the pursuit of their ideal. The architecture of the palaces that surround the square is mostly in 1800's style, as in the National Museum (1885-1890) that rises with its great neo-renaissance structure behind Saint Venceslas monument (where the square used to be closed by the Horses Portal, demolished in 1875). The sumptuous marble interiors house anthropology, natural history, mineralogy and archeology exhibitions. A superb example of Art Nouveau architecture is instead the Hotel Evropa (1903-1906), decorated inside and out with every motif that could possibly be conceived in this charming art style. On the opposite side of the National Museum, on the right corner of the square is located the Koruna Palace, in a style of Babylonian inspiration, so called for the crown that is set on its tower. On the left are found the Peterka House, remarkable example of secession style, the Whiel House, that the architect Antonín Whiel in the 19th century built for his own residence, with its wonderfully frescoed façade; and finally the elegant Oil Lamp House, designed by the architect Václav Havel, grandfather of the president of the Republic.

View of Venceslas Square, equestrian monument of Duke Venceslas, and National Museum

Loretto

Founded by Catherine of Lobkowitz at the beginning of the 17th century, this Sanctuary is one of the most extensive and massive architectural complexes of the city, built around the Holy House, a replica of the Virgin Mary's home that the legend says was brought by angels in flight from Nazareth to Loretto, in Italy, at the end of the 13th century. Decorated outside with events of Mary's life, the Chapel was built right after the battle of the White Mountain (1620) and soon became one of the symbols of the victory of Catholicism over the Protestants. In the following years, a richly frescoed cloister was built around the house, together with other monuments of the sanctuary. The façade, designed in baroque style by the famous architects Dientzenhofer, is decorated by sculptures inspired to the Annunciation. The core of the building rises toward the sky with a bell tower in baroque style containing the famous Peter Naumann (1694) music box that plays at each hour a different tune. Among the numerous chapels of the complex, the baroque Church of the Nativity, with its rich frescos, sets itself apart for proportion and elegance. In the Treasury of the sanctuary are preserved jewels and precious items (the chalices and ostensoria, in particular, are splendid), priceless contribution of the nobility of Prague.

1. Detail of the tower clock
2. The Loretto Sanctuary is a complex of baroque buildings. The famous music box made of 27 bells is located on the tower
3. Interior of the Loretto Sanctuary
4. The replica of the Holy House (1621-1631) at the center of the Loretto Sanctuary complex
5. Street lamp

Charles Bridge

1. *Charles Bridge: 10 m. wide and 520 m. long, it is completely made of sand stone*
2-3. *A group of statues on Charles Bridge*

With its 500 meter length, the bridge crosses the Vltava and the tiny island of Kampa, uniting Staré Mesto, the Old Town founded around the 11th century, to Malá Strana, the Small Neighborhood grown between the 13th and 18th century at the foot of the Castle Heights. Peter Parléř, architect of the cathedral of Saint Vitus, received from Charles IV in 1357 the commission to build it to replace the preceding Judith Bridge, destroyed by a violent flood 15 years before, in 1342. The latter had been built in stone on order of the Queen Judith, wife of Vladislav I, to replace in its turn a wood bridge of very old date (935) that was parallel to the present one. The construction, supported by 16 massive pillars, was realized between 1357 and 1401 in sand stone, and till the 1800's held the record for being the sole stone bridge over the Vltava. Crowded day and night by people and stand of all kinds (in the last years it is a pedestrian area) it is famous mainly for the sculpture groups that decorate it. The monuments line up between the two portals of the bridge, which were built in different periods, but both in gothic style. The one toward the Old Town was constructed at the same time as the bridge, by Parléř, in the shape of a powerful defensive tower. Designed by the same architect, the outside decoration includes valuable sculptures,

including the portrait of Charles IV, Venceslas IV and St. Vitus. On the upper floor is the elegant Gallery of the Tower, offering a unique view of the city. The portal on the side of the Small Neighborhood, instead, was built in the early 1400 at the side of a lower tower, remainder of the Judith Bridge, and another one built 50 years later, similar to the Parléř's tower, but soberer. Mostly replaced by copies (the originals being held in the Lapidarium of the National Museum), the statues of the bridge were added to the original three that decorated the bridge since its building: the Crucifixion, St. John Nepomuk and the Pietà. Starting from the Old Town tower, on the right side are found first the 18th century groups with the Madonna, St. Bernard and the Virgin with St. Dominic and Thomas of Aquinas. Next is the Crucifixion, that replaced in 1630 the original sculpture lost at the time of the Hussite Wars. Curious detail is the golden inscription in Hebrew "Saint, Saint, Saint is the Lord", which the legend says was donated by a Jew in 1696, who was forced to pay for it in reparation for having violated the Cross. Past the four statues of Saints, the bronze monument of St. John Nepomuk, the most ancient on the bridge (1683) is found; it depicts the martyrdom of the Saint, one of the most revered in Prague, thrown in the Vltava in 1393 for order of Venceslas IV.

Passing beyond the other saints figures and reached the portal of the Small Neighborhood, the visitor re-

1. *A group of statues with Castle in the background*
2. *The Tower toward the Old Town: the portal with the insignia of the countries linked to the Bohemian Crown*
3. *Charles Bridge, Towers toward Malá Strana and in the background the Church of St. Nicholas*
4. *Charles Bridge*
5. *Procession*
6. *Charles Bridge at night*

Page 50-51 The Bridges of Prague

turns back, meeting at his right, after the statue of St. Venceslas, the 18th century group called "the Turk of the Bridge", representing also St. John of Matha and St. Felix while freeing the Christians held prisoners by the Heathens. Next are the statue of St. Adalbert and the group of the Mystical Vision of St. Luitgard (1710), deeply expressive and artistically significant. Here are found the stairs that lead to the Kampa Island. Beyond them and the statue of St. Nicholas of Tolentino, the group with the Saints Vincent Ferrer and Prokop, and behind it the copy of a 1500's statue of a horseman, are met. Among the remaining sculptures is St. Francis Xavier, on which side the sculptor Brokoff placed a self-portrait.

1. *The majestic cathedral of St. Vitus*
2. *Novotneho Lavka*
3-4. *The Tour Boats propose unforgettable cruises on the Vltava. Kampa island seen from Charles Bridge*
5. *Charles Bridge and St. Salvator Church seen from the Vltava bank*
6. *Street artists*

1. The massive bronze chariot on a pillar of
   the main front of National Theater
2. National Theater

National Theater

Out of more or less thirty stages presently found in Prague, the National Theater is certainly the most famous and beloved by Prague's and foreign public, both for the artistic and architectural value of the building that houses it, the quality of the shows that are held in it, and the symbolic meaning it has assumed in the history of the Czech art and culture. The Theater was actually born because of the nationalistic drive already expressed at the end of the 18th century by the movement of the Reawakeners, a group of intellectuals committed to the promotion and defense of the Czech national culture. The determination and ambition of the Czechs to possess their own national stage brought in 1849 to the decision to take steps for building the theater, requiring of course a great sum of money. The Austrian Administration was deaf to any request for financing, but the Czechs did not let it stop them. In May 1868, thanks to the substantial funds collected with a popular subscription in all the Czech territory, the corner stone was laid. The works were directed by the architect Josef Zítek. The generosity and dedication of the Czechs were not rewarded though: in summer 1881, few weeks after the inauguration of the theater, the building was completely destroyed by a fire. The reconstruction was accomplished in record time, only two years, once again financed by the spontaneous donations of the population. The architect was Josef Schulz, who also built the National Museum. To the wonderful decoration of the exterior and interior contributed all the major Czech artists of the end of the 19th and beginning of the 20th century. In the decade 1970-1980 the theater underwent a thorough restoration that included, with the construction of the New Stage, the addition of a new wing with auditorium and services (restaurant, bar and cafe), created in glass by Karel Prager according to the most contemporary architectural trends: here are held the famous shows of the "Laterna Magika". In the old building, composed of

1

2

many levels, the center portion of the façade presents a loggia with five arches below a terrace with a balustrade decorated with statues of Apollo and the Muses. The wings support bronze statues of the winged Victory on a chariot. The theater is covered by a stunning blue dome studded with stars. The interior is richly decorated, with a refinement already clearly affirmed in the Grand Foyer, graced by fanlights painted by Mikoláš Aleš with allegorical scenes from Smetana's opera "Má Vlast" (My Homeland), or in the paintings in the Women's and Men's Halls. The most impressive interior is the great Hall of the Auditorium, though, with its ceiling bearing symbolic figures of the arts and the curtains painted by Hynais in red and gold, illustrating the popular collection of funds for building the theater. Equally remarkable are the sumptuous royal box (become later the presidential one), replete with gold and velvet, and the precious crown of three nows of boxes, gallery and balcony overlooking the stage. In November 1983, at the reopening of the theater after restoration, in the Auditorium was performed Smetana's opera Libuše, the very same that a century before opened the artistic activity of the National Czech theater.

1. *Night view of the National Theatre*
2. *National Theater: built in the years from 1868 to 1881 in the neo-renaissance style of northern Italy*

Map

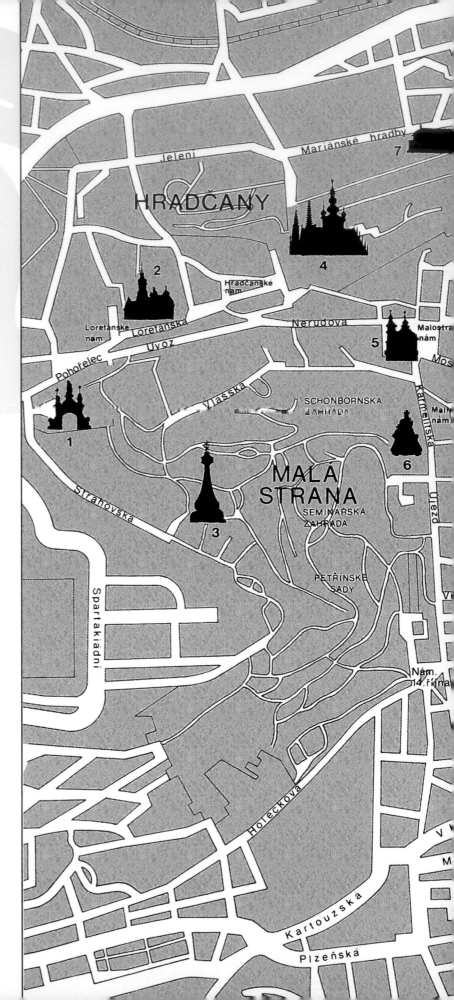

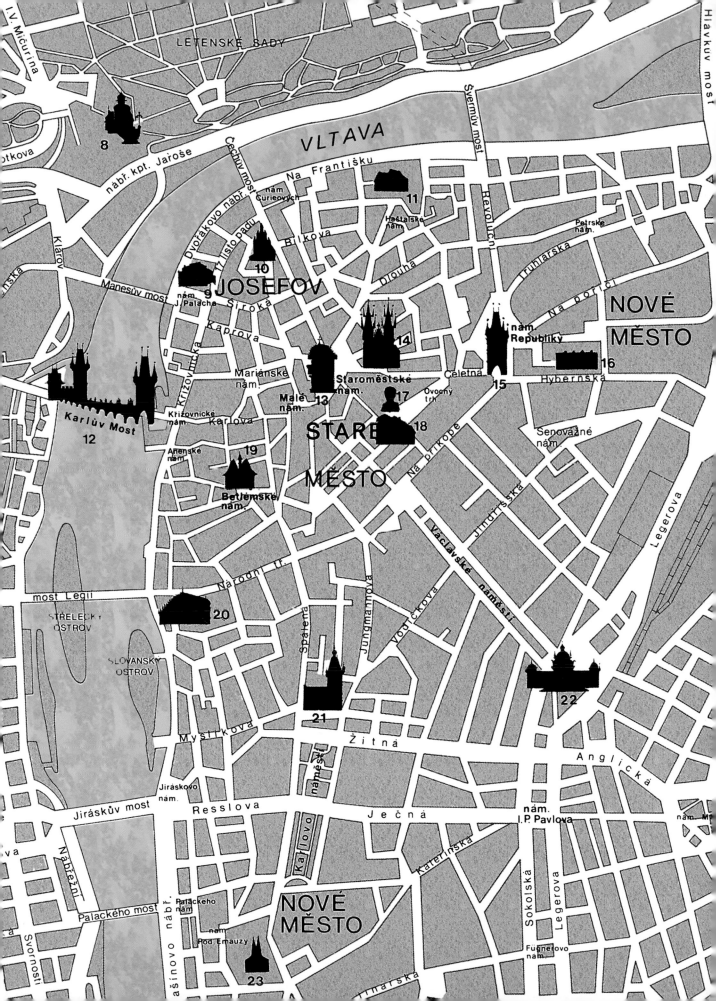

Index

© KINA Italia / L.E.G.O. S.p.A.

Texts: Claudia Converso
Translation: A.B.A. - Milan
Design and printing: KINA Italia / L.E.G.O.